BUDDHISM
Learning to Understand Life

Nina van Gorkom

March 2026

First published in January 2024.
Reissued in March 2026.
Zolag
www.zolag.co.uk

ISBN 9781897633502

Contents

Nina van Gorkom 1928-2023

Nina van Gorkom died peacefully in her sleep on December 31st, 2023 aged 95. Below is a letter written by her good friends Sarah and Jonothan Abbott.

In memory of Nina van Gorkom

A reflection on behalf of those who knew Nina through a shared interest in the Dhamma.

Nina was a very dear friend to all those who shared her interest in the Buddha's teaching (the Dhamma). Nina was much admired for her writings, for her detailed knowledge of the texts (scriptures), and for her positive contribution over almost 60 years to the discussions with Ajahn Sujin. Ajahn Sujin is the person who has been our guide in understanding the Buddha's teaching as found in the original texts. For many of us, Nina's writings were our first experience of an explanation of the Buddha's teachings in writing that was meaningful and relevant to our ordinary daily life. Some of us have been fortunate to know Nina well for a very long time and to frequently travel with her.

Nina's enthusiasm for putting in writing what she was studying and for sharing this with others was extraordinary. Her body of work included:

- Records of her many trips with Ajahn Sujin and the group to India, Sri Lanka and other places. These were narrative reports in which Nina had skilfully woven the important parts of the discussions, making use of the extensive notes and audio recordings she made during each trip.
- Reference works cover the more detailed aspects of the teachings, many of which were not otherwise available. The preparation for these required considerable research and a knowledge of the ancient Pāli language (in Nina's case, this was self-taught).
- Translations from the Thai language of books written by Ajahn Sujin. These works included important reference material that was not then available to the English speaking world.
- Extensive writings on a myriad of topics on the internet forum 'Dhamma Study Group', over the past 20 years.

Nina's scholarship and research skills were impressive, as was the volume (and speed) of her output. In total she wrote some 16 books and 22 articles, and translated 4 works from the Thai. These have been translated into numerous foreign languages. We are extremely grateful for this legacy.

Some time after the loss of her dear Lodewijk, Nina resumed travels to Asia on her own, and she continued these even when assistance with mobility became necessary.

Since Covid struck and weekly Zoom discussions with Ajahn Sujin began, Nina has been a regular participant. She was usually the first to speak each week, bringing up topics that she knew would be useful for everyone. We last had the pleasure of her company online on the day before she passed away. We will miss Nina's cheery presence, keen interest and good friendship. Our condolences to her family members.

Sarah and Jonothan Abbott, 6 January 2024

Words of the Buddha from the sutta 'A Single Excellent Night'*:

"Let not a person revive the past
or on the future build his hopes;
For the past has been left behind
And the future has not been reached.
Instead with insight let him see
Each presently arisen state;
Let him know that and be sure of it,
Invincibly, unshakeably.
Today Death may come, who knows?"

* *MN 131, Translated by Bhikkhu Ñāṇamoli and Bhikkhu Bodhi*

Preface

It is difficult to understand the truth of life. The Buddha taught what life really is. It is said that the Buddha's birth was on the full moon day of Vesākha (May) 623 B.C. His teachings are preserved in the scriptures, which are the Suttanta, the Vinaya or Book of Discipline for the monks, and the Abhidhamma. These are called the Tipiṭaka. After the Buddha's passing away, the Great Councils were held where the teachings and commentaries to them were rehearsed together by a group of five hundred perfected ones (arahats). The first Council was held shortly after the Buddha's passing away, the second Council one century later, and there was a third Council. The ancient commentaries date from the first Council. Nine centuries after the Buddha's passing, the great Commentator Buddhaghosa wrote an encyclopedia, the "Visuddhimagga" (Path of Purification), and he and other monks compiled commentaries from earlier texts to the Tipiṭaka.

I am using some terms of the Pāli language, the language of the scriptures called Theravāda. You may be used to Sanskrit terms such as dharma, karma, and prajna, but in Pāli the words dhamma, kamma, and paññā are used. Most important are not the terms but what their meaning is in our life at this moment.

In this book, I also quote from some of my discussions with Ajahn Sujin, a wise Dhamma friend who always helps people understand the Buddha's words. I am happy to share with you what I learned from her and my other Dhamma friends. Discussions about the Buddha's teachings help us to consider more deeply what he taught us, the truth preserved in the scriptures even after many centuries.

India became very dear to me when I visited the holy places with Ajahn Sujin and other friends countless times. The holy places are Lumbini, where he was born; Bodhgaya, where he attained enlightenment; Sarnath, where he began to teach Dhamma; and Kusināra, where he finally passed away.

During our pilgrimages in India, we talked about the Buddha's life and about the perfections he accumulated as a Bodhisatta in the course of innumerable lives. This is also a way of paying respect to the Buddha. Contemplating the Buddha's perfections can remind us to consider the reality appearing at the present moment. At each place, we discussed the perfections—the wholesome qualities such as liberality, sīla (good morality), patience, or determination to continue considering the truth of the teachings. We also have to develop the perfections since they support the development of understanding of the truth the Buddha taught. If we have only theoretical knowledge of the Buddha's teachings acquired from reading, we cannot understand what he taught. During our pilgrimage to the holy places, we talked about the eye, seeing, and visible object; the ear, hearing, and sound; and about the other realities appearing all the time in daily life, to have right understanding of them.

1

What is life?

The Buddha taught what life is. We think of life as the whole lifespan of a living being from birth to death. Actually, life is only one moment of experiencing. It is changing all the time. And it is now. We may be seeing now, and then life is seeing. Or we may be thinking about what is seen, and then life is thinking. We see and hear pleasant and unpleasant things; nobody can change this since each moment has its proper conditions. We tend to forget that each experience is extremely short. It seems that it was already there for some time and that it lasts a while. In reality, each moment, be it pleasant or unpleasant, wholesome or unwholesome, just arises for an extremely short while and then it is gone immediately, never to return.

We find our life very important, but life is only one moment in the endless series of experiences that come and go. There is actually birth and death at each moment which arises and then falls away immediately. The last moment of this life is immediately followed by the first moment of the next life, and so the endless cycle of birth and death goes on and on.

We read in the commentary to the "Basket of Conduct" ("Khuddaka Nikāya") about the many lives of the Bodhisatta before he awakened to the truth and became the Buddha:

> "In his life, when the Bodhisatta was Yudanjaya, he was the eldest son of the King and had the rank of viceroy. He fulfilled every day mahā-dāna, the giving of an abundance of gifts. One day he visited the royal park; he saw dewdrops hanging like a string of pearls on the tree top, the grass tips, the end of the branches, and the spiders' webs.
>
> The prince enjoyed himself in the royal park, and when the sun rose higher, all the dewdrops hanging there disintegrated and disappeared.

> He reflected thus: 'These dewdrops came into being and then disappeared. Even so are conditioned realities, the lives of all beings; they are like the dewdrops hanging on the grass tips.' He felt a sense of urgency and became disenchanted with worldly life, so he took leave of his parents and became a recluse."

Seeing now is not the same as seeing a moment ago. Seeing arises, and then it falls away, never to return, like the dewdrops, and this is life. We still have an idea that seeing can stay, that it is always there and that it is "my seeing." Seeing and all our experiences are mental realities that appear in our life. Seeing is actually a moment of consciousness that experiences what is visible, a visible object. Hearing is another moment of consciousness that experiences sound. Smelling experiences odour, tasting experiences flavour, body consciousness experiences a tangible object, and through the mind all kinds of objects can be experienced.

A moment of consciousness is called in Pāli citta. At each moment in life, there is another citta or consciousness that knows an object, and there can be only one citta at a time. Seeing cannot arise at the same time as hearing; they experience different objects. Seeing experiences a visible object through the doorway of the eye, and hearing experiences sound through the doorway of the ear. Cittas experience different objects through the doorways of the eye, the ear, the nose, the tongue, and the mind. A doorway is the means through which citta experiences an object. There are six worlds: the world appearing through the eyes, through the ears, and the other senses and the mind. We think of a mind that coordinates all our experiences, but this is an illusion. There is not one mind that stays, a mind we take for "my mind," but there are only different cittas that arise one at a time and fall away immediately. We think of our whole body, but this is only an idea. When the body is touched, hardness may appear, and hardness is a reality that can be directly experienced. At such a moment, there is no clinging to our whole body. What we take for self or "me" are only different mental elements and physical elements that arise and fall away. That is the meaning of the Buddha's teaching of non-self.

From birth to death, life is an unbroken series of cittas that succeed one another. The last moment of life is succeeded by the first moment of the next life. Even so, the first moment of this life has succeeded the last moment of the past life.

We read in the "Discourse Collection" (Sutta Nipāta, translated by John D. Ireland, "The Arrow", Wheel Publication 82):

> "Unindicated and unknown is the length of life of those subject to death. Life is difficult and brief and bound up with suffering. There is no means by which those who are born will not

> die. Having reached old age, there is death. This is the natural course for a living being. With ripe fruits, there is the constant danger that they will fall. In the same way, for those born and subject to death, there is always the fear of dying. Just as the pots made by a potter all end by being broken, so death is (the breaking up) of life.
>
> The young and old, the foolish and the wise, all are stopped short by the power of death, all finally end in death. Of those overcome by death and passing to another world, a father cannot hold back his son, nor relatives a relation. See! While the relatives are looking on and weeping, one by one each mortal is led away like an ox to slaughter.
>
> In this manner, the world is afflicted by death and decay. But the wise do not grieve, having realized the nature of the world. You do not know the path by which they came or departed. Not seeing either end, you lament in vain. If any benefit is gained by lamenting, the wise would do it. Only a fool would harm himself."

Each life is like this and evolves according to specific conditioning factors beyond our power. Through the Buddha's teachings on life and death, we can learn that there is, in reality, no person or self who can be master of life. It needs courage and sincerity to accept the truth.

There is a great variety of cittas. They may be wholesome, unwholesome, or neither wholesome nor unwholesome. They may be results of kamma, a good or evil deed performed in the past. The moment of birth, for example, is the result of kamma, in Pāli vipāka, and also during life the moments of seeing, hearing, and the other sense impressions are results of kamma performed in the past. Vipākacittas are neither wholesome nor unwholesome. Thus, wholesome or unwholesome cittas are cittas that are cause; they may motivate good or evil deeds, whereas the cittas that experience pleasant or unpleasant objects are cittas that are results, vipākacittas. We cannot choose whether there will be a happy rebirth or an unhappy birth, whether we see or hear pleasant or unpleasant objects, or whether wholesome cittas or unwholesome cittas arise because of what is experienced. All kinds of cittas that arise do so because of their appropriate conditions, and they are beyond control. This teaches us that no self can control life's events.

Pleasant events and unpleasant events in our lives alternate, and our reactions are different. Sometimes cittas that are good and wholesome arise, for example, when we are patient and we think of the benefit of others and try to help them. Sometimes we are overcome by aversion and think of ourselves; we are sorry for ourselves. When there are problems in our work or our relationships, we blame others. We blame our circumstances, the weather, disease, or the government. We may wonder what type of citta arises: is the citta wholesome or unwholesome? Cittas succeed one another extremely rapidly, and it is hard to know when the citta is wholesome and when unwholesome.

For example, a mother may believe that she has only unselfish love for her child, but is there no selfish attachment? The moment she thinks of the benefit of her child is different from the moment she enjoys the company of her child. Citta arises only for a moment, and there is a different citta all the time. Nobody can force himself not to enjoy pleasant objects, but understanding can be developed of the different moments that arise in our life. All these moments arise because of their proper conditions.

It is difficult to understand the truth of non-self because clinging to self is deeply rooted. I had a conversation with Ajahn Sujin about this subject:

Ajahn Sujin: We can just say: there is no "I", but understanding of anattā must be developed. When we do not think of another person, he is not there. When seeing arises, no other person is experienced. The world appears, but actually, one citta at a time arises and falls away. Because of the wrong remembrance, one takes what is experienced as permanent.

Nina: I do not really grasp it that there is no person, only nāma dhammas and rūpa dhammas.

Ajahn Sujin: You have to listen more and then you will have more understanding.

Nina: But it takes a long time before we understand the truth.

Ajahn Sujin: Each day dhamma is dhamma. We have dear people, people who are close to us, but dhamma arises and then falls away. Seeing has fallen away, and there is nothing left. Thinking, all dhammas fall away completely. This is not different from the moment a dear person dies. We are thinking about a dear person, but thinking falls away completely.

Everything is dhamma now. Understanding depends on conditions. We are inclined to think of concepts about people and events. If there are conditions for the arising of sati (mindfulness), it can know the characteristics of realities. There can be right understanding that all dhammas are anattā.

Nina: It is so difficult.

Ajahn Sujin: Surely, paññā (understanding) can arise and accumulate. It is not a matter of 'doing something' but of understanding. Everyone would like to have paññā, but the moment of understanding is paññā. When a reality appears, paññā can know the truth. Do not try to have it. At this moment it can be known to what extent paññā has developed.

When we say that the Dhamma is difficult to understand, Ajahn Sujin explains that at such a moment we are praising the Buddha. He had to develop understanding for countless lives to know the true nature of all that appears in life and to teach us today. His first utterance after his enlightenment was that the Dhamma is difficult to understand and that it goes against the stream of common thought. We read in "The Connected Discourses of the Buddha" (translated by Bhikkhu Bodhi, Part I, Ch 6, 1) that the Buddha said after he attained enlightenment:

> "Enough now with trying to teach
> What I found with so much hardship;
> This Dhamma is not easily understood
> By those oppressed by lust and hate.
> Those fired by lust, obscured by darkness,
> Will never see the abstruse Dhamma,
> Deep, hard to see, subtle,
> Going against the stream."

The Brahmā Sahampati entreated him to teach Dhamma.

We can have confidence in his teaching because the Buddha would not have taught the Dhamma if it was impossible to develop an understanding of the truth. But the development of understanding is bound to take innumerable lives.

2

What is suffering?

When a dear person dies, it is very natural to have grief because of one's loss. But grief does not last. When one feels the loss of a dear person through death, one is thinking of oneself; one regrets that one no longer enjoys their company. It is good to know that we mostly cling to ourselves.

We read in the "Kindred Sayings" (15:3, Tears, Assu Sutta, translated by Ven. Bodhi):

> "For a long time, bhikkhus, you have experienced the death of a father... brother... sister ... son... daughter... the loss of relatives... the loss of wealth... loss through illness; as you have experienced this, weeping and wailing because of being united with the disagreeable and separated from the agreeable, the stream of tears that you have shed is more than the water in the four great oceans. For what reason? Because, bhikkhus, this saṁsara is without discoverable beginning... It is enough to experience revulsion towards all formations, enough to become dispassionate towards them, enough to be liberated from them."

Saṁsara means the cycle of birth and death. Life after life there are birth and death; one has to suffer the loss of relatives, of wealth, and loss of health through illness. This moment now is a moment of saṁsara.

Only one citta arises at a time, but it is accompanied by different mental factors, in Pāli: cetasikas, that support the citta in knowing an object at that moment. Citta cannot arise alone, by itself. Citta and cetasika arise together, experience the same object, and fall away together, but they are different. Now there is seeing. Citta is the chief at the moment of experiencing. It arises just to experience an object. The cetasikas that accompany citta have each their own characteristic, their own function.

The accompanying cetasikas condition seeing-consciousness to see, such as the cetasika that is contact, phassa. We see this and hear that because of phassa. Citta is the principal, the leader, in knowing an object, and the accompanying cetasikas experience the same object, but they each perform their own function. Some cetasikas accompany each citta, such as contact and remembrance (saññā); some accompany only unwholesome cittas, and some accompany only wholesome cittas.

Feeling is a cetasika accompanying each citta. Feeling may be happy, unhappy, or indifferent. Feeling has no possessor; nobody can choose what feeling arises. If it is time for an unhappy feeling, nobody could make it a happy feeling; it is non-self, anattā. Some people believe that happy feeling is always wholesome, but this is not the case. When one has a happy feeling at the moments of listening to music or enjoying the company of friends, there is attachment and this is unwholesome. When someone with true compassion assists others, there may be a happy feeling that is wholesome. Kusala cittas and akusala cittas alternate very quickly, and only highly developed paññā knows their difference.

Wholesome qualities like unselfish love and unwholesome qualities like aversion or anger are actually different cetasikas: unselfish love arises with wholesome cittas, and aversion or anger with unwholesome cittas. Some unwholesome and wholesome cetasikas are roots (in Pāli: hetu or mūla) because they are the foundation of the unwholesome or wholesome citta, like the root of a tree that sustains its life.

There are three unwholesome roots: attachment, aversion, and ignorance. We are attached to all objects experienced through the senses and the mind. We want to go on seeing visible objects, hearing sound, and touching all tangible objects. We cling to life, to persons, and mostly to ourselves. We have aversion when we experience unpleasant objects through the senses, when the events of life do not evolve according to our expectations, or when we meet people who do not behave as we think they should. Ignorance is ignorance about the truth of life, of the impermanence of all that occurs because of the appropriate conditions, of the nature of anattā of what is alive and what is not alive. Whenever an unwholesome citta arises, it is either rooted in attachment and ignorance or aversion and ignorance or ignorance alone. Ignorance is the root of every unwholesome citta.

There are three wholesome roots that are the opposites of the unwholesome roots: non-attachment, non-aversion, and understanding or wisdom. When we are generous and want to support others, there are the wholesome roots of non-attachment and non-aversion, and these arise with every wholesome citta. At such moments, we do not think of our own benefit or gain, but we are concerned about the welfare of others. The wholesome root of understanding does not arise with every kusala citta, but when there are the right conditions, it may arise. We should remember that understanding is not "self". It is a cetasika that can only arise when there are conditions. Listening to the words of the Buddha as we find them in the teachings, wisely considering what we read or what we hear during discussions about the Dhamma, are conditions for the growth of understanding. If we try to follow a specific method, or seek a quiet place that seems more favourable for the development of understanding, we are drifting further and further away from the truth of non-self that the Buddha taught. Our actions and thoughts are time and again motivated by clinging to an idea of self, and this is not known.

Besides unwholesome roots and wholesome roots, there are many other akusala cetasikas and beautiful cetasikas that accompany akusala cittas and kusala cittas. One may like to be peaceful and calm, but in spite of one's wish, there is restlessness and worry. One can learn from such experiences that there is no self who could exert control over the different cittas that arise in a day. The Buddha taught many details of citta and cetasikas with the aim to show the nature of anattā, non-self, of all conditioned realities.

The gradual development of understanding is in the scriptures (Gradual Sayings, Book of the Sevens, Ch VII, § 7) compared to the wearing out of a knife handle one holds each day, yet it wears away so slowly that one cannot perceive it happening. Ignorance and wrong view have been accumulated for countless lives.

Cittas can be accompanied by many different kinds of cetasikas and they experience different objects in a day. Seeing experiences all that is visible, a visible object; hearing experiences sound; tasting experiences flavour. When we are enjoying a delicious meal, there are different kinds of cittas, such as tasting-consciousness, citta with attachment, and thinking of flavours. Only one type of citta arises at a time. Tasting-consciousness experiences flavour. Visible object, sound, or flavour are different physical phenomena and these are different from mental phenomena, nāma. They are rūpa; they do not experience anything, but they are experienced by citta and cetasikas, by nāma.

When we hear a dog barking, different moments of experience arise. Hearing hears that particular sound, and then we remember that it is the sound of a dog. It is not "I" who remembers but saññā, remembrance or perception, a cetasika which remembers an object or "marks" it so that it can be recognized later on. Saññā accompanies each citta, be it seeing or hearing or the citta which thinks of concepts. We recognize people and things because of saññā. Previous experiences are remembered. Also, in the past, the sound of a dog was heard; we learned what a dog is and the way it barks. There is no dog in the sound. It is only rūpa which impinges on the ear-sense; when there are the right conditions, a particular sound, pleasant or unpleasant, can be heard.

The Buddha taught what nāma and rūpa are—all phenomena that appear—so that we could learn their true nature of non-self. We read in "Kindred Sayings" (IV, SN 35:26, III, The All) that the Buddha said at Sāvatthī:

> "Bhikkhus, without directly knowing and fully understanding the all, without developing dispassion towards it and abandoning it, one is incapable of destroying suffering.
>
> And what, bhikkhus, is that all without directly knowing and fully understanding which, without developing dispassion towards which and abandoning which, one is incapable of destroying suffering?
>
> Without directly knowing and fully understanding the eye, without developing dispassion towards it and abandoning it, one is incapable of destroying suffering. Without directly knowing and fully understanding forms... eye-consciousness... eye-contact... and whatever feeling arises with eye-contact as condition... without developing dispassion towards it and abandoning it, one is incapable of destroying suffering.
>
> Without directly knowing and fully understanding the ear... sounds... ear-consciousness... ear-contact... and whatever feeling arises with earcontact as condition..."

He said the same about all other phenomena appearing through the other senses and the mind.

Suffering is a translation of the Pāli term dukkha. It is not merely what we mean by suffering in conventional language. In its deepest sense, it is the unsatisfactoriness of all conditioned phenomena that do not stay, that arise and fall away. We would like to experience only what is pleasant, to meet only friendly people who speak kind words to us, but there is no self who can arrange anything in life. Whatever happens does so according to the proper conditions. It is due to past kamma whether we experience pleasant objects or unpleasant objects. We cannot do anything, we never know what will happen the next moment; there may be an accident, or death may occur. This reminds us that being in the cycle of birth and death is dukkha. Most of the time we are forgetful and we go on enjoying life. Paññā that has been developed can really understand the danger of birth.

While I was discussing with Ajahn Sujin about old age and loss of dear people, a friend, whose wife was ill with cancer, had entered the Foundation. Ajahn Sujin spoke to him with great compassion:

"Dukkha is heavy. Nobody likes it. It is a danger; it causes citta to be sorrowful, troubled. Nobody is freed from it, but we must understand it. When we have more understanding of the Dhamma, we shall see that what arises must fall away; this cannot be altered.

Birth is really troublesome. We have to eat to stay alive; we have to see; there is no end to seeing. Seeing is a burden because, through seeing, there is attachment. Is seeing beneficial, or is it a danger and disadvantage? When there is seeing, there will be clinging to what is seen. We are searching for the things we like, but if we do not search for what we like, we live more at ease. From where comes the burden? From seeing and from wanting the things we see. We can come to understand that each citta that arises and falls away is a burden. Everything that arises and falls away is great dukkha."

The sutta that was just quoted above teaches us that in order to make an end to dukkha, the eye, visible object, and seeing have to be directly known and fully understood and that detachment from them has to be developed. We have to know seeing as it is. It cannot arise if there is no eye-sense and no visible object. It cannot arise when kamma does not produce it.

Dukkha is often translated as suffering, but this word does not cover all its different meanings. Different aspects of dukkha are explained in different contexts of the teachings.

Bodily pain and mental unhappy feeling are dukkha everyone experiences. One feels unhappy about getting what is not wanted and not getting what is wanted. Does this not happen very often in life? We expect kindness from others, but instead, it seems that people are indifferent or even unkind to us.

Furthermore, there is dukkha in change, the changeability of happy feeling. We may enjoy with happy feeling agreeable company, a beautiful landscape, a comfortable home, bodily well-being without sickness or pain, but these occasions for happy feeling do not last; happy feeling soon comes to an end.

Dukkha, in its deepest sense, is dukkha inherent in all conditioned realities that arise and fall away at every moment. What is impermanent cannot be a refuge; it is unsatisfactory. This kind of dukkha is the first Noble Truth. The second Noble Truth is the cause of dukkha, which is clinging. So long as there is clinging to the phenomena of life, there are conditions for birth again and again. There will be the arising and falling away of realities again and again, which is dukkha. The third Noble Truth is the end of dukkha. When understanding of realities has been fully developed, enlightenment can be attained and then defilements are eradicated stage by stage. Wrong view has to be eradicated first. So long as we take realities for self, there cannot be a lessening of other defilements. Before we realize it, an idea of self who wishes for progress arises and that is not the Buddha's Path. When all defilements have been eradicated there is no condition anymore for rebirth, and that is the end of dukkha. The development of understanding of the realities of life is the Path the Buddha taught and is the fourth Noble Truth.

It is possible to develop the Path leading to the end of dukkha, but it will take countless lives. However, a beginning can be made now by understanding the different characteristics of realities that appear. Seeing is a mental reality, hardness is a physical reality, and these have different characteristics that can be investigated. What we call our body are different kinds of rūpa which arise and fall away. We think that we have arms and legs, but what can be directly experienced? When we touch what we call a body, hardness may appear—no arms and legs, because these are only in our thinking. Hardness appears just for a moment and then it falls away immediately. Where is the body? An image of a whole body that exists is just in our thinking. We are attached to our body and want it to be without sickness and pain, but it is not possible to exert control over our body. There are only different bodily phenomena, rūpas like hardness, cold, heat, that arise because of their proper conditions.

3 Processes of citta

Rūpa does not know or experience anything. We think that rūpas of the body can feel pain, but it is nāma, the cetasika feeling, that feels pain. Rūpas arise and fall away in groups or units of rūpas. Each group consists of several kinds of rūpas, which always include four kinds of rūpas which are called the four Great Elements: the Element of Earth or solidity, appearing as hardness or softness; the Element of Water or cohesion; the Element of Fire or temperature, appearing as heat or cold; and the Element of Wind, appearing as motion or pressure. Solidity, temperature, and motion or pressure are objects which can be experienced through the body-sense, whereas cohesion can only be experienced through the mind-door.

Rūpa does not think, it cannot feel, it cannot remember, but it can be experienced by citta. There are several kinds of rūpa, and among these, seven rūpas are experienced all the time in daily life. These are: visible object, sound, odour, flavour, and the tangible objects which are solidity, appearing as hardness or softness; temperature, appearing as heat or cold; and motion, appearing as motion or pressure. If there were no citta, nothing could appear; there would not be the world.

Cittas which experience objects through the doors of the senses and the mind arise in a process or series of cittas. When, for example, hearing arises, it occurs within a series or process of cittas, all of which experience sound. Rūpa lasts longer than citta and cetasika, and thus, several cittas can experience rūpa that has not fallen away yet. Only hearing-consciousness hears, but the other cittas within that process, which is called the ear-door process, do not hear, but perform their own function while they still experience the sound. Hearing-consciousness is vipākacitta, result of past kamma. After hearing-consciousness has fallen away there are, within that process, akusala cittas or kusala cittas which experience the sound in an unwholesome or wholesome way.

When we are at a concert and listen to beautiful music, we are likely to be attached to sound. Or there may be kusala cittas which realize that sound is only a kind of rūpa. When we hear the loud sound of traffic on the street, we are bound to have aversion. Cittas succeed each other very quickly, and we may not know that there are different series or processes of cittas experiencing an object through the eye-door, the ear-door, the nose-door, the tongue-door, the body-door, and the mind-door. After the cittas of a sense-door process have fallen away, the object is experienced by cittas arising in a mind-door process, and after that process has been completed there can be other mind-door processes of cittas which think about what was experienced.

When we learn about cittas arising in different processes and experience different objects, it helps us to understand more that there is, in reality, no self, no person who could control the events of life. There is no person, and what we take for different events of life are in reality only different mental phenomena and physical phenomena which take their course according to their proper conditions. Nobody could change the order of cittas arising in a process. They arise and fall away, never to return.

The Buddha taught many details of citta, cetasika and rūpa, with the aim to help us to understand the truth of anattā.

We read in the "Kindred Sayings" (III, §33 (1), "Not Yours"), that the Buddha, while he was at Sāvatthī, said:

> "What do you think, monks: if people were to carry away the grass, sticks, branches and leaves in this Jeta Grove, or burnt them or did with them what they pleased, would you think: These people carry us away, or burn us, or do with us as they please?"
>
> "No, Lord."
>
> "Why not?"
>
> "Because, Lord, that is neither our self nor the property of our self."
>
> "So, too, monks, give up what is not yours! Your giving it up will for a long time bring you welfare and happiness. What is it that is not yours? Corporeality... feeling... perception... mental formations... consciousness are not yours. Give them up! Your giving them up will for a long time bring you welfare and happiness."

Ajahn Sujin said, as I quoted before, "When we do not think of another person he is not there." This may be hard to grasp. At the moment of seeing, only what is visible is experienced, and there is no thought of anything else. It is only when we think of another person that he is there in our thoughts. We are used to thinking of persons as permanent, but this is imagination. Ajahn Sujin explained: "You think a lot of someone, and where is that being? Only a story in your mind. You make it up by thinking. The previous experiences condition the thought of someone, some being."

Seeing sees visible object, and after seeing has fallen away we pay attention to shape and form, and this is not seeing but thinking. It is important to reflect on the difference between seeing and thinking of concepts such as people and things.

We may not realise how extremely brief one moment of citta is. When there is seeing it seems that we immediately see people, but then seeing has fallen away and thinking has arisen already.

When thinking arises it is always either kusala citta or akusala citta. We may believe that so long as we do not commit strong akusala kamma there are not many akusala cittas arising. However, the more we study the Dhamma the more we come to know that there are countless akusala cittas arising in a day. When we are not generously giving things away, assisting others, being respectful to others, abstaining from evil deeds, developing true calm that is wholesome, or developing understanding of the truth the Buddha taught, the citta which thinks is unwholesome.

Wise people, also before the Buddha's time, saw the danger of attachment to sense objects and learnt to develop true calm which is wholesome. They did not choose to develop calm; it was right understanding that conditioned detachment and the development of calm. Calm is a wholesome cetasika arising with each kusala citta. Whenever kusala citta arises there is also the cetasika calm. But it does not last; it falls away with the kusala citta. If there is understanding that knows the right conditions for the development of tranquil meditation or samatha, there can be more moments of true calm. This cannot be developed without understanding of what is wholesome and what is unwholesome and of the way to attain true calm by means of specific meditation subjects like the Buddha's excellent qualities or death.

If one just wants to be calm without there being paññā that sees the danger of attachment, it is impossible to develop calm. Some people take for calm what is only a feeling of relaxation with attachment. There are many misunderstandings about what one takes for calm and about the way to develop calm. People want to escape from unpleasant situations; they wish to be without anger and unpleasant feeling. They believe that being in a quiet place and concentrating on one object will help them to be calm, without disturbance. They believe that this is meditation, but they do not know that this is attachment, not the development of samatha. Samatha is a way of mental development, bhāvanā, and there cannot be any mental development without understanding.

In Pāli, the word bhāvanā stands for mental development. There are samatha bhāvanā and vipassanā bhāvanā which are different ways of development, each with a different aim. The aim of samatha is temporary freedom from clinging to sense objects, whereas the aim of vipassanā is the eradication of all defilements.

Also, before the Buddha's time, samatha was developed by those who had accumulated conditions to develop calm to a high degree—the degree of jhāna or absorption—so that they could become free from sense-cognitions and from being enslaved to them. By the development of samatha defilements can only be temporarily subdued; they are not eradicated. By the full development of vipassanā, defilements are eradicated stage by stage. Vipassanā is taught only by the Buddha. It is clear, direct understanding of whatever reality appears at the present moment. This understanding eradicates ignorance, wrong views and all other defilements.

So long as there are ignorance and wrong view, there are conditions to be born again and again and there will be dukkha again and again. It seems that we are going around in a vicious circle, clinging to the five khandhas, conditioned realities, again and again. Only right understanding can eventually lead to the end of dukkha.

We read in the "Kindred Sayings" (III, Khandha vagga, Middle Fifty, Ch V, par. 99, The Leash) that the Buddha said at Sāvatthī:

> "Just as, monks, a dog tied up by a leash to a strong stake or pillar, keeps running round and revolving round and round that stake or pillar, even so, monks, the untaught manyfolk... regard body as self, regard feeling, perception, activities, consciousness as self... they run and revolve round and round from body to body,

> from feeling to feeling, from perception to perception, from activities to activities, from consciousness to consciousness...they are not released therefrom, they are not released from rebirth, from old age and decay, from sorrow and grief, from woe, lamentation and despair...they are not released from dukkha, I declare"

It is so fortunate that we are still able to learn what the Buddha taught about realities so that the truth can be realised very gradually.

Cittas arise and fall away in succession so rapidly that it seems that cittas such as seeing and thinking of what is seen occur at the same time, but in reality there are different types of citta arising in different processes. We believe, for example, that we see a table, but in reality there is a process of cittas experiencing visible object through the eye-sense, and then there is a process of cittas experiencing visible object through the mind-door, and later on there are other mind-door processes of cittas which think of the idea of a table. A table cannot be directly experienced; it is only an idea constructed by thinking. A concept is not a reality, but the thinking of concepts is real; it is citta which thinks.

Whatever appears does so because of its proper conditions. Nobody can choose or select what appears now. When it is the right time for seeing, attachment, or understanding, they appear, and their characteristics can be known one at a time.

Seeing sees visible object, but it lasts only for an extremely short moment and then it is gone. Visible object does not last either; it falls away. Seeing can only see; it cannot think of visible object. If one wants to concentrate on seeing or visible object, if one has any idea of fixing one's attention on them with the purpose of knowing them, it prevents right understanding of realities. We cannot stare at visible object, since it is seen just for a moment, and then it falls away. We may think about it, but that is not direct understanding of its characteristic when it appears.

Insight, direct understanding of realities, is developed in stages and the first stage clearly distinguishes nāma from rūpa. This level of understanding may seem to be far away, but it is useful to know that this is the first stage. Otherwise, one may mistake thinking for direct understanding. When one experiences changes of the body temperature or notices the appearance and disappearance of sound, one may believe that one experiences the impermanence of rūpas. However, the arising and falling away of nāma and rūpa is the fourth stage of insight, which cannot be realised if the first stage has not been reached: clearly knowing nāma as nāma and rūpa as rūpa.

Life exists only in a moment. When we consider this more we shall be less inclined to cling to the idea of a thing or a person. When we cling to someone or dislike someone, it is only thinking. We always think of people, but when understanding arises, the characteristic of thinking can gradually be known as a conditioned reality.

Intellectual understanding (pariyatti) can condition later on direct understanding of realities (paṭipatti). Pariyatti is not theoretical understanding; it is understanding of what appears now. When pariyatti has become very firm it can condition direct understanding of realities appearing at the present moment. Then there will be clear understanding that in reality there are only ever-changing mental phenomena and physical phenomena. That does not mean that we cannot lead our ordinary life with all the ideas of persons and things. We lead our life naturally, but with more understanding of what is really there for a split second. We go along with all our usual activities in daily life, paying attention to the people around us and to the tasks we have to perform, but in between there can be a moment of understanding the true nature of any reality that appears now, be it seeing, aversion or sound; understanding it as a conditioned reality that is not self.

4

Citta, cetasika and rūpa

It is helpful to consider again and again the following verse of the "Mahā-Niddesa" quoted in the "Visuddhimagga" (VII, 39):

"Life, person, pleasure, pain - just these alone
Join in one conscious moment that flicks by.
Ceased aggregates of those dead or alive
Are all alike, gone never to return.
No [world is] born if [consciousness is] not

Produced; when that is present, then it lives;
When consciousness dissolves, the world is dead:
The highest sense this concept will allow" (Nd.1,42).

Life, person, pleasure, pain: What is that? It is all that appears through the five senses and the mind-door. When seeing arises, life is seeing; when hearing arises, life is hearing; when thinking arises, life is thinking. When we think of a person, he seems to exist, but what we take for a person are only impermanent nāma and rūpa, fleeting phenomena. Pleasure and pain are impermanent: in our life happy moments and sad moments alternate, they appear one at a time. We attach great importance to our experiences in life, to our life in this world, but actually, life is extremely short, lasting only as long as one moment of citta.

As we read:

"No [world is] born if [consciousness is] not
Produced; when that is present, then it lives;
When consciousness dissolves, the world is dead."

When we are thinking about the world and all the people in it, we only know the world by way of conventional truth. It seems that there is the world full of beings and things, but in reality there is citta experiencing different dhammas arising and falling away very rapidly. Only one object at a time can be cognized as it appears through one doorway. Without the doorways of the senses and the mind the world could not appear. So long as we take what appears as a 'whole', a being or person, we do not know the world.

If there were no citta, nothing could appear, but since citta arises at each moment, realities appear. We are reminded of the brevity of all experiences, including thinking with worry about our problems. The real cause of problems is not in the outside world nor in other people, it is in the citta.

People wonder what they should do in difficult situations, in their dealings with other people. They ask: "What next?" But who knows the next moment? This depends entirely on conditions which are beyond control. Because of our clinging to the idea of self we create our own problems and we believe that we can be acting in this or that way to solve our problems. The development of right understanding of one reality at a time as it appears at this moment is the condition that one will be less taken in by concepts and ideas of the conventional world with all the problems and worries. One begins to see the world in the ultimate sense: citta, cetasika and rūpa. That is the world that really matters, that is the world that should be understood more and more.

People may wonder how to solve problems. Some people think that this could be with therapy. Ajahn said:

"Is there a problem now? What is the cause of problems?"

The Dhamma is not like a therapy. The cause of problems is that we are thinking of self, that we relate problems to ourselves. Problems cannot be solved by clinging to an idea of self. All that is arising now is only a conditioned dhamma, not self, and nobody can make it arise or do anything about it. When we listen to the Dhamma there can be a little more understanding. The development of understanding is with ups and downs but we can see that even a little more understanding is beneficial. We cannot expect an immediate result of listening and considering the Dhamma. When there is any expectation, we cling to an idea of self. We should accept that the development of paññā is just step by step.

Sarah, one of our friends who always helps explain the Dhamma, said that one learns to live easily and naturally while developing understanding instead of trying to change one's life with the wrong idea of self. She said: "It is like letting go of a big burden. The happiness of understanding is different from the happiness with clinging."

The development of understanding should be with courage and gladness. Ajahn Sujin told us to be happy about the reality that appears. She said: "Be happy. Whatever occurs is just a moment, and it does not last. It is only a reality that has fallen away completely and is no more." We should be grateful that the Buddha taught that whatever appears is only a conditioned dhamma, impermanent and not self.

Is there seeing now? What we take for a person is only visible object that is seen for an extremely brief moment.

While realities are considered in the right way, there is no worry, no disturbance at that moment. Ajahn Sujin said:

"Everyone clings to what one takes as real when (actually) it's not real, it's like a dream. We consider this life so very important, but it will be like a dream for the next life. So what about yesterday - happiness, enjoyment, clinging - they're gone, so it's like a dream. It seems so important, but actually, it's not - it's only thinking about people and things. For the whole life, there may be no understanding of realities at all, and not just one life, many, many lives. This is the path - the developing of understanding - otherwise, there are no conditions for right understanding at all because right understanding must be unexpectedly arising by conditions, pure conditions."

It is essential to know the difference between what is real in the conventional sense and what is real in the absolute or ultimate sense. If we only know conventional truth and do not know ultimate truth, the clinging to the concept of self and all other defilements cannot be eradicated. Notions such as person, world or tree are conventional truth, they are concepts we can think of, but they are not real in the ultimate sense. Mental phenomena or nāma and physical phenomena or rūpa are ultimate realities or paramattha dhammas. They have each their own unalterable characteristic, they are real for everybody; the names of realities can be changed but their characteristics are unalterable. Nāma is the reality which experiences something, whereas rūpa does not experience anything. Seeing, for example, is nāma; it experiences visible object which is rūpa. We may change the names "seeing" or "visible object", but their characteristics cannot be changed. Seeing is real for everybody, anger is real for everybody, no matter how we name it. A person is not real in the ultimate sense; what we take for a person are ever-changing nāmas and rūpas.

Citta can experience an object through eyes, ears, nose, tongue, body and mind-door. Before we heard the Dhamma it never occurred to us that only one object through one doorway at a time is experienced. We used to think of an impression of a whole like a person. Then life goes on with ignorance, day after day—thinking of what is not real. Now we learn that through eyes only what is visible is experienced, no person. We have to consider this often before it sinks in.

Sarah said: "It takes a lot of courage to accept and understand that there is no more to life than the citta now. All the past experiences we treasure so much, all the future dreams, all our ideas about our dear ones... all just at this moment, this citta now which thinks this way or that on account of experiences through the sense doors."

Ajahn Sujin writes in her book "A Survey of Paramattha Dhammas" (Ch 16, Citta):

"... Someone may be unhappy and he may worry about it that he is growing older and that sati arises very seldom. When one worries, the citta is akusala. We should not because of the Dhamma have akusala cittas, we should not be worried. The Buddha taught the Dhamma in order that people would be encouraged to apply it, develop it with perseverance and be inspired by it. Akusala arises when there are conditions, there is no self who can prevent its arising. When akusala citta has already arisen, we should not be downhearted, but we can take courage if there can be awareness of the characteristic of akusala which appears... One will not be troubled about akusala if one does not take it for self."

When understanding of the Dhamma is developed through listening and considering the present reality, sati arises with paññā that is of the level of intellectual understanding. Sati is a wholesome cetasika that is non-forgetful of what is wholesome. It accompanies each kusala citta. Sati can be of different levels, of dāna, of sīla, of samatha and of vipassanā. When there is an opportunity to be generous in giving or assisting someone else, we may be lazy and forgetful so that it is impossible for us to be generous or to help. When sati arises it is non-forgetful of the opportunity for kusala such as generosity and mettā. When intellectual understanding of the Dhamma is being developed sati is non-forgetful of the reality that appears at the present moment, but there are not yet direct awareness and direct understanding. Intellectual understanding can, when it has become firm, condition direct understanding of the reality that appears. At that moment there are direct awareness and direct understanding of whatever reality that presents itself. This is different from thinking about realities.

Sati is not awareness or mindfulness, as we use these words in the conventional sense. It is not knowing what one is doing, like walking or focusing on an object. One should know what the object of sati is: any object that appears at the present moment by conditions. It is not a situation or a concept but a reality like sound, hardness, attachment or thinking. There should not be any selection of specific objects; also unpleasant objects and unwholesome objects can be known one at a time when they appear. That is the only way to understand that whatever appears is anattā; it is not in one's power to have any control. If one believes that the situation is not favourable for sati or that one should create conditions for sati one is on the wrong Path leading one further away from the truth.

Anger or attachment can be objects of mindfulness. They may arise because these realities also arose in the past. They arose and fell away with the citta but they are accumulated from one moment of citta to the succeeding moment of citta, from life to life. Kusala and akusala lie dormant in each citta and when there are conditions they can arise.

When we see it, we think that we are in this world, a world full of people, houses, and streets. When we hear, we think that we are in this world, we hear people, animals, cars. We think all the time of the whole wide world with people and things in it. In reality, there is only one moment of seeing, one moment of hearing, one moment of thinking.

Seeing sees just what appears through eyes, visible object, and then both seeing and visible object fall away. After that we think of a person or of the whole world, because saññā remembers. There is only one moment of hearing and then both hearing and sound fall away, but we keep on thinking about what was heard, because saññā remembers.

When we think of a person or of the world, the object of citta is a concept. As soon as we notice the shape and form of a person or a thing there is a concept of a "whole". Even when we do not think of names we can still have a concept as object. When we perceive a pen we know already a concept before we think about the name "pen". Children who cannot talk yet and who do not know the meaning of conventional terms which are used in language can know concepts of a "whole". When they grow up they learn conventional terms so that they can name different things. They can then understand which person or thing is referred to. The English word "concept" (in Pāli: paññatti) stands for the idea which is the object of thinking as well as the name or term used to denote such an idea.

We should not try to avoid thinking of concepts; even the thinks of concepts because there are conditions for thinking. The Buddha knew who Sariputta was but he had no wrong view about "person". The does not cling to concepts, but we are still clinging. We have not eradicated "attā-saññā", the wrong remembrance of things as "self". We cling to the general appearance of things and to the details. When we cling to the image of a man or woman, we do not know the reality which appears through the eyes, a visible object, and, thus, we know only a concept, not a reality. We do not only like the general appearance of things, we also like the details. We are attached to the trademark of clothing, of cars.

There are conditions to think of concepts, of "wholes", we need conventional terms in order to communicate with other people. We should lead our daily life naturally, but we can develop understanding of citta, cetasika and rūpa in our daily life. One may believe that these are constituents of a whole, but where is that whole? It only exists in our thinking; it cannot be directly experienced. We think that we see people lifting their hands or walking, but in reality there are countless nāmas and rūpas arising and falling away. So long as we do not realise the arising and falling away of nāma and rūpa, we cling to the idea that what appears are people, women or men, or this or that thing. We cling to the concept of somebody or something.

Many conditions are necessary for the arising of direct understanding, such as reading, discussing and considering the characteristic of whatever reality appears at the present moment. When we remember that intellectual understanding of the present reality, pariyatti, can become firmer by the appropriate conditions, we shall be less inclined to force the arising of direct awareness and understanding. If one tries hard to make direct awareness arise one thinks that there is awareness, but it is not right awareness. We may mistakenly think that there is direct awareness of realities when we are only clinging to an idea about awareness, or to an idea of a self who can have awareness at will.

The Buddha taught satipaṭṭhāna or the "applications of mindfulness". Under these applications realities are classified as bodily phenomena, feelings, cittas and dhammas. These are, in fact, all realities that naturally appear in daily life and can be known as they are. Sati of the level of satipaṭṭhāna is direct awareness of the reality appearing at the present moment. It accompanies paññā and then the reality which appears can be known as only a conditioned dhamma that is not self or mine. If one does not know about the different levels of intellectual understanding and direct understanding one may take thinking of realities for direct awareness of the level of satipaṭṭhāna. One is likely to be attached to an idea of self who thinks. The wrong view of self is deeply ingrained and one may not realise it when it arises.

Now follows an interview about the Abhidhamma, given to my Dutch friends.

The word Abhidhamma is often used for the third book of the scriptures that consist of Sutta, Vinaya and Abhidhamma. However, actually, Abhidhamma means dhamma in detail, everything that is real and can be known at this moment. Each reality appearing at this moment is actually Abhidhamma, such as seeing, visible object, anger or understanding. The terms Abhidhamma, paramattha dhamma (ultimate reality) or just dhamma denote reality that can be known now, no matter where one is or what one's activities are.

Interview about Abhidhamma

Question: Can you say in short what is the Abhidhamma?

Nina: The Abhidhamma explains what life is. Before hearing the Buddha's teachings we had different ideas about life. Life is only one moment and it changes all the time, it falls away immediately. At the moment of seeing, life is seeing, at the moment of hearing, life is hearing. The Buddha explained about all that can be experienced through the senses and the mind.

We always thought that life is permanent and that there is a self coordinating all experiences. The Buddha explained that there is no self, only momentary realities that change all the time. What we take for a person are different mental moments and physical moments. None of these moments can stay and they cannot be controlled, they cannot be caused to arise.

Question: How did you come into contact with the Abhidhamma?

Nina: I came to Thailand and met Ajahn Sujin. I was looking for something but did not know what. I thought that there must be something else apart from parties and all the things that keep us busy in daily life. She explained that vipassanā, insight into what is real, can be developed in daily life. Since I had a very busy life I thought that I could not retire and stay in a quiet place. She took me to the provinces, outside Bangkok, and explained to me simple things in the situation of daily life. For example, when we worry or have problems, these are only moments of thinking. She did not wait to explain to me about nāma, mental phenomena, and rūpa, physical phenomena. She explained that these are different kinds of reality. Nāma can experience something and rūpa cannot experience anything, but it can be experienced. She explained realities as they occur in different situations. Situations are not realities. We think of people and things but actually there are only nāma and rūpa. We can think of situations, ideas, concepts, and thinking itself is a reality.

Question: How did you begin studying the Abhidhamma?

Nina: By reading suttas and listening to Ajahn's radio programs. I listened each morning during breakfast. In this program she explained about citta, a moment of consciousness, that arises within a process or series of cittas. She enumerated each of these moments of citta that succeed one another, explaining this every day again and again. In this way one could learn about the processes of citta.

Asking questions I found important. Every time I visited Ajahn, I had a whole list of questions. She also made me work, writing about Dhamma. She had an English program and every fortnight there had to be a new program. I had to think it over and write down what I had reflected on. That was very helpful for the development of understanding.

Question: It was a favourable condition that there was a teacher near you. What advice do you have for others who want to begin with the study and do not have a teacher near them?

Nina: The Buddha said all the time that one should listen to the Dhamma and consider what one hears. This can also be done by reading the texts, but that is not sufficient. Discussion helps, such as we do at our online meetings, asking questions, discussing and reflecting on what one has heard. There are no other means than these.

Question: The Abhidhamma often deals with consciousness, and what is the meaning of consciousness, citta?

Nina: Before coming into contact with the Buddha's teachings we always thought of a self who coordinates all experiences, such as I see, I think, and we believed that also the brain plays its part. The Buddha's teaching is quite different. There are specific conditions for each moment of citta. The visual object and eye-sense are conditions for seeing; they associate so that seeing can arise. At the same time, seeing is the result of a former deed or kamma. There are many types of citta. Seeing and hearing are results of kamma, deeds committed in the past. We see and hear agreeable objects or disagreeable objects; seeing and hearing are results of good deeds and evil deeds. Then there are reactions to these experiences; these are more the active side of our life. We can react with wholesome consciousness or unwholesome consciousness, and this is also conditioned. It is conditioned by accumulations of former experiences. Because of our education, what our parents taught us, there may be wholesome moments of generosity, moments of assisting others, and such good qualities fall away immediately together with consciousness. But each moment of consciousness conditions the following consciousness and that is why good and bad qualities can be passed on. They are never lost; they are passed on from one moment of consciousness to the next one, from one life to the next life. That can be called accumulation, the accumulation of good and bad qualities in consciousness. Such accumulations are among others a condition for the way we react to sense impressions.

Question: The book you wrote about the Abhidhamma is called Abhidhamma in Daily Life. Can you elaborate more on what the Abhidhamma means in daily life?

Nina: The Abhidhamma helps one to know oneself, but what we call self are actually changing moments of consciousness. The aim of the Buddha's teaching is not having more wholesomeness and less unwholesomeness. The aim is understanding, understanding that whatever arises is conditioned. It cannot be controlled, but it can be understood. One often reacts to whatever occurs with attachment or with aversion, and these have arisen already. It is not possible to make them disappear, but they can be understood as conditioned elements, thus, as non-self.

Question: Can you say more about feelings and emotions?

Nina: We find feelings about our different experiences so important. We think of my feelings, my problems. It means that we are engaged with ourselves.

Feeling in the Buddha's teachings is different from emotions as we see them in the conventional meaning. Feeling is only a mental factor, cetasika, which accompanies each citta. Its function is tasting the object that is experienced by citta. There are not only pleasant feeling and unpleasant feeling, but also indifferent or neutral feeling. Seeing now is accompanied by indifferent feeling. We believe that there is at that moment no feeling, but there is indifferent feeling and it falls away immediately. Feeling is a reality that is quite different from what we consider feeling in the conventional sense. We are very attached to feeling and our ideas about feeling, but actually it is only a cetasika that falls away immediately.

When we have problems in life we find them very important, but in fact these are only moments of thinking with different cetasikas such as aversion which falls away immediately. We believe that we can control them but in the end they are solved in a way that is totally different from what we expected. I experienced that during my journey. I was worried about my travelling which I find so difficult. I was reminded by a friend that in that way I was occupied with myself. I could not have any control. They were always solved in a way beyond expectation. I was worried about how I could manage without a walker when arriving in Thailand and Vietnam. But there were walkers when I arrived; people had given them to me. I could not have known this ahead of time.

Sarah had given me very good reminders about worry. She had just had an accident, an electrical shock, because of touching an electric device. She was flung from one side of the room to the other side. Shortly afterwards, she spoke very helpful words to me to remind me of the truth while I was worrying, but afterwards, she could not remember what she had said. Those were kusala cittas that conditioned her speaking. It was beyond control.

Question: We always want to experience agreeable emotions. Can you add something about that?

Nina: When we do not have them as expected, we are disappointed. One cannot control anything and one has to accept that.

I heard during our sessions about people who awoke during the night because of fear, but that is not in accordance with the Buddha's teachings. Following his teachings should lighten one's burden, not add to it. One cannot control whatever happens, but one can come to have more understanding. The Path of the Buddha does not have anxiety as effect.

Question: But we all have fears. How should we see these in accordance with the Abhidhamma?

Nina: By not taking them for self or mine. Only a mental reality, not self. One can never know the next moment.

Question: Alertness or paying attention is a very important factor.

Nina: This word may be misleading. We need a word that is a translation of sati, but alertness could suggest a self who is alert and notices whether a reality is wholesome or unwholesome. It may give an idea of a self who notices this. Sati is a cetasika that can only arise with a wholesome citta. It is non-forgetful of what is wholesome. There are many levels of sati, such as sati that is non-forgetful of generosity. We may have an opportunity to help someone else, but we are lazy and do not move. But when sati arises because of conditions, it remembers that helping is wholesome and then we will help others. That is only one level. There is also sati of a higher level. There are many different realities, such as seeing, thinking of what is seen, and attachment, and then there is the realisation that understanding these realities is beneficial. It is not self that realises this; it is sati. Sati is mindful, non-forgetful, of whatever reality appears. Sati may arise or may not arise; we do not know ahead of time, we cannot arrange for it.

Question: Which were the four points that were mentioned during your journey as conditions for understanding?

Nina: Listening to the teachings, and this can be by means of discussion or reading. Considering what one hears—thus, it is not merely passive listening. One does not have to do this deliberately, but later during the day, for example, there may be conditions to recall what one heard or read and reflect upon this. These are two points. The third point is that considering the Buddha's words is to be in daily life. It is not necessary to go to a specific place. It has to be in daily life. While we are talking or in the kitchen, we can consider the Dhamma we heard. The fourth point is confidence: confidence that this is the Buddha's word and that we can develop an understanding of what he taught.

Question: Are these four points helpful to establish sati?

Nina: We should not have an idea that it is necessary to establish sati. It depends on conditions whether or not sati arises. What is most important is not alertness but understanding the different moments of consciousness and the physical phenomena, nāma and rūpa. This is the aim, and it can condition later on direct understanding of realities through satipaṭṭhāna. We should not have expectations. When we have expectations, there is already attachment. Whatever attachment there may be, it is counterproductive.

Glossary

- **Abhidhamma**: Means "dhamma in detail," referring to the analytical doctrine of the scriptures and every reality that is real and can be known at this moment.
- **Akusala**: Defined as unwholesome, demerit, sin, bad action, or unskilful.
- **Anattā**: Non-self or soul-less; the truth that all mental and physical elements are ownerless and arise only by conditions.
- **Anicca**: Meaning impermanent, not stable, or that which does not stay.
- **Arahat**: One who has attained the "Summum Bonum" (final liberation) and does not require further training.
- **Bhāvanā**: Mental development, which includes the development of calm (**samatha**) and the development of insight (**vipassanā**).
- **Bodhisatta**: One who is destined to become a Buddha.
- **Cetasika**: A mental factor or property that arises with consciousness, experiences the same object, and performs a specific function.

- **Citta**: A moment of consciousness; it is described as the principal or chief reality which experiences an object.
- **Dāna**: Generosity, giving, or the bestowing of alms.
- **Dhamma**: A broad term encompassing reality, the natural law, the Teaching of the Buddha, doctrine, or truth.
- **Dukkha**: Suffering, pain, or the inherent unsatisfactoriness of all conditioned phenomena that arise and fall away.
- **Hetu**: A root or foundation for wholesome or unwholesome consciousness, acting like the root of a tree.
- **Jhāna**: A state of mental absorption or concentration of mind developed to a high degree through **samatha**.
- **Kamma**: Deed or action; specifically the intentional volition that motivates acts and produces results (**vipāka**).
- **Khandha**: An aggregate, mass, or group; any conditioned reality—physical or mental—that arises and falls away.
- **Kusala**: Wholesome, good action, merit, virtue, or clever.

- **Mettā**: Amity, benevolence, or loving-kindness.
- **Mūla**: Root or foundation, used synonymously with **hetu** in the context of mental states.
- **Nāma**: Mental phenomena or the immaterial factors of life; the reality that experiences something.
- **Paññā**: Understanding, wisdom, or insight into the true nature of realities.
- **Paññatti**: A concept, name, or term used to denote an idea; it is the object of thinking but not an ultimate reality.
- **Paramattha dhamma**: Ultimate reality; things like **nāma** and **rūpa** that have unalterable characteristics and are real for everyone.
- **Pariyatti**: Intellectual right understanding of reality, or the scriptures and code of the Holy Texts.
- **Paṭipatti**: Direct understanding of reality.
- **Phassa**: Contact; the mental factor that conditions the mind to experience an object.
- **Rūpa**: Physical phenomena, material composition, or matter; realities that do not experience anything but are experienced by **nāma**.

- **Saṃsāra**: The cycle of birth and death, often described as having no discoverable beginning.
- **Saṅkhāra**: Volitional formations or conditioned things; it refers to things that construct or are constructed.
- **Saññā**: Perception, memory, or recognition; the mental factor that "marks" an object so it can be recognized later.
- **Sati**: Mindfulness or awareness; a wholesome mental factor that is non-forgetful of what is wholesome or the present reality.
- **Satipaṭṭhāna**: Applications of mindfulness; the practice of direct awareness of realities as they appear at the present moment.
- **Samatha**: Tranquil meditation or the way of concentrating the mind to temporarily subdue defilements.
- **Sīla**: Morality, moral practice, or code of conduct.
- **Vipāka**: Result, fruition, or consequence; consciousness that is the result of past **kamma**.
- **Vipassanā**: Insight; wisdom which sees realities as they are and leads to the eradication of all defilements.

Books by Nina van Gorkom

- *The Buddha's Path.*
- *Buddhism in Daily Life.*
- *Abhidhamma in Daily Life.*
- *Cetasikas.*
- *The Buddhist Teaching on Physical Phenomena.*
- *The Conditionality of Life.*
- *Letters on Vipassanā.*
- *A Survey of Paramattha Dhammas.*
- *The Perfections Leading to Enlightenment.*
- *An Introduction to the Buddhist scriptures.*
- *Understanding Realities Now: Nina's Travelogues.*
- *The World in the Buddhist Sense.*
- *Understanding Life Now*, by Sarah Procter Abbott and Nina van Gorkom.

More details on these books can be found at: www.zolag.co.uk and alwell.github.io/Support/

www.ingramcontent.com/pod-product-compliance
Lightning Source LLC
La Vergne TN
LVHW030923080826
845145LV00013B/3024

* 9 7 8 1 8 9 7 6 3 3 5 0 2 *